SPEED UP YOUR
COMPUTER'S
SPEED
BY
300%

SIMPLE & EFFECTIVE WAYS TO BOOST YOUR COMPUTER'S SPEED

By William Hill

Table of Contents

RECOMMENDED RESOURCES

Don't Lose Your Digital Life. Back Up All Your Data, Music & Photos Files For FREE   http://bit.ly/freedatabackup

Fix The Blue Screen Of Death On Your Pc - http://bit.ly/FixBlueScreenOfDeath

Computer Repair Video Course - Learn How To Repair Your Computer & save Money On Costly Repairs And Even Start Your Own Business http://bit.ly/ComputerRepairMastery

Laptop Repair Made Easy (Hd Video Series) - Laptop Repair Made Easy Is A Complete High Definition Video Series On How To Repair Laptops For Fun Or Profit http://bit.ly/LaptopRepairMadeEasy

Lcd Monitor Repair Made Easy - How To Repair Lcd Monitors With Step-by-step Videos - http://bit.ly/LcdMonitorRepairMadeEasy

Filecure Instantly Fixes All Types Of Broken Or Unknown File Extensions Including Unknown Email Attachments, Archived And Compressed Files, Audio And Music Files, Document Files, Internet Downloads, Graphic Files, Movies Videos, Multimedia Files, And More - http://bit.ly/FileCure101

Regcure - #1 Registry Cleaner. - http://bit.ly/RegCureClean

Best Data Recovery Software - Data Recovery Software Products for All Windows and Mac Computers - http://bit.ly/DataRecoverySoftware

Xoftspyse - Clean Spyware Instantly - The New And Improved Xoftspyse Is The Most Powerful Anti-spyware Program Yet. Promote This Fresh New Gui, A Suite Of Advanced Features, The Largest Spyware Detection Database, Lighting Fast Free Scan - http://bit.ly/Xoftspy

Scan And Fix Windows Errors Fast - Thoroughly Scans Your PC For Errors. One Click And PC Unleashed Fixes Them All. Tools To Repair And Optimize - http://bit.ly/FixWindowsErrorsFast

Getting Started

First things first, I want to thank you for buying this book and I know that if you are reading this book, my guess is that you fall into one of these few categories of pc users. Perhaps you have recently purchased a new PC or laptop that works just fine, but you would like it to be even faster.

You may have bought the pc for general home or office use, or perhaps for something even more specific like browsing the web, displaying high-end graphics or gaming. It may also be that what you have is an older PC or laptop that used to work alright before now but now operates at snail speed.

Over time, computers get congested with so many files and applications like the temporary internet files, unused software and all kinds of digital rubble.

The good news is that there are several steps and procedures that you can take to de-clutter your pc and give it a major boost in it's operating speed. That is the essence of this book. Some of the steps are very simple and do not require the assistance or consultation of a computer engineer while others require specialized software applications in order to perform them.

It must also be mentioned here that, depending on your level of experience with working with computers, it might be a good idea to consult an expert if you don't know what you're doing. The last thing you want is to cause permanent damage to your computer and your files. So, If in doubt, call in an expert.

From freeing up storage space on your hard disk to backing up your data files, this book will give you the fundamentals on the best pc maintenance activities that will help keep your computer running smoothly and in tip-top shape. These step-by-step procedures will also show you how to scan for viruses, malware and spyware lurking on your computer and also how to clear your computer's cache.

You will learn simple tips for cutting through all the clutter and the end of the day, you will end up with a PC that boots up much faster, runs more smoothly and crashes less often, if at all.

No matter your level of experience with computers, they will eventually slow down over time. It's just the nature of the beast. Luckily, there are quite a few simple methods we can use to help speed them up again; mostly without the need to upgrade our computer's hardware.

Now, depending on the version of Windows that you have installed on your pc, you can either choose to use the free automated tools and resources from Microsoft Corporation to trouble-shoot and resolve the issues that are slowing down your computer or you could decide to follow the steps outlined below to identify and fix the issues on your own.

Before we begin, you need to consider this one minor detail; is the slow speed from your PC or from your broadband connection?

In other words, is it your PC or your internet connection that is slow? If, for the most part, you mostly use your PC for surfing the web, sending emails and such, there is a possibility that your internet connection is the culprit and not your PC. If you're still not convinced, you could easily check the speed with a broadband speed checker like the one offered by PC Advisor.

Likewise, if what you have is a laptop computer, you can test it with your neighbor's fast broadband connection (if they let you) or try it on your office connection if you have a good broadband speed. If after taking either one of these steps the situation is the same, then the problem lies with your pc.

On the other hand, if what you own is a desktop computer, then you can easily borrow a friend or colleague's laptop just to perform the same check at home. If the borrowed laptop computer still runs slowly, then you can safely conclude that the network connection is the problem.

Now that we have established the cause of the problem, the next logical step to improve the situation would be to complain to your ISP. Their technical department will help you sort it out.

Once that is done, you can then continue to apply the following steps outlined below.

However, another word of caution is necessary here. Please, for your own sake, do not do anything to your computer that is beyond the scope of what is outlined here. Whenever you are in doubt or you find yourself way in over your head, ask for help from a more technically savvy person so that you don't cause irreparable damage to your computer.

That said, you can take the following easy steps outlined below to begin;

If you are a more advanced computer user, I recommend that you download a free tool from the Microsoft website that shows you every single one of the programs and processes that run on your computer each time you launch Microsoft Windows. This also includes the programs that Windows itself needs to be able to operate successfully on your pc.

CAUTION – You should use this tool only if you are an advanced user who is capable of restoring Windows after an error occurs. Most procedures for boosting computer speed discussed in this book can be stopped midway to avoid causing damage to your PC. Cautiousness and good judgment are very important whenever you're working with computers.

Automated Solution

One other tool I recommended is 'Microsoft Fix'. It is a 100% free tool that can automatically diagnose and trouble-shoot for you and help improve your pc's performance. This tool is designed to resolve many of common issues that pc owners experience. Some of these include:

- Power saver settings solution

- Multiple anti-virus software programs running on the same device

- Unnecessary programs running at startup

- Insufficient hard drive space

- Too many unused programs

- Leftover programs

- Old, very large cached

- numerous temporary internet files

- Too many programs running in the background

- Data corruption/corrupt data programs

- Hard disk fragmentation/fragmented disk

- Missing Windows updates or outdated drivers

Note: Microsoft Fix it is currently NOT AVAILABLE for Windows 8.1 and Windows 8. (However, it may have become available for those operating systems depending on when you're reading this book)

Steps to Improving Your Computer's Performance

The following steps outlined below can be performed to improve your computer's performance. For best results, these steps should be performed in order.

Alternatively, you can decide to perform the simplest and least invasive steps first if you don't want to mess around too much with your pc's settings and configurations. You could choose to do the easiest steps first until your system starts performing better.

a) Limit number of programs that run at start-up

Anytime you boot your pc, there are a lot of programs that start to run automatically in the background with or without your knowledge. Running too many of such programs will definitely hinder your computer's performance as those other programs use up the computer's resources like the RAM and hard disk.

To limit the number of programs that run in the background, first take these steps to learn what's running when you boot your computer:

1. Click the **Start** button, type **System Configuration** in the search box, and then click **System Configuration** in the list of results.

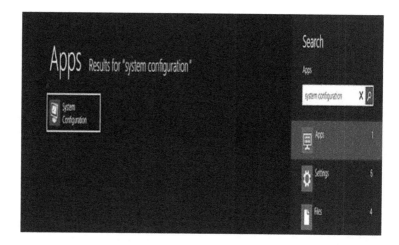

2. Click on the **Start-up** tab. The programs that are set to run automatically at start-up are indicated with a check mark. You can clear the check boxes for any programs you don't want to run in order to disable them. However, you need to ensure that you only disable the programs that you're familiar with. You don't want to disable the essential programs

3. that Microsft Windows need in order to run successfully. Once again, if you're in doubt, PLEASE don't clear the check box.

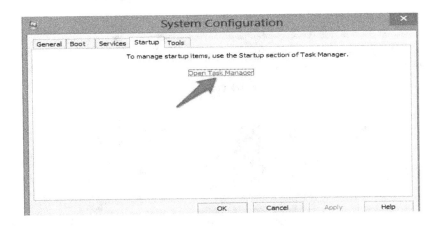

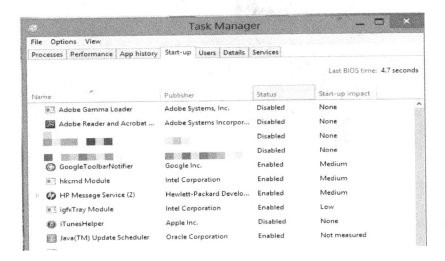

b) Delete, delete, delete

Any PC that is not clogged up with too many programs will surely be a fast computer. This implies that if you want a faster pc, your best bet is to uninstall all the installed programs that you don't use at all or that you only use occasionally.

You need to delete stuff like any trial software, limited-edition versions, and anything else you're never going to use or whose license has expired on your pc. To uninstall any bit of software on your PC, perform the following steps:

1. Click the **Start** button, and then click **Control Panel**.

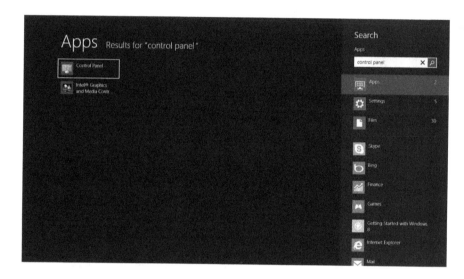

2. Under **Programs**, click **Uninstall a program**. (If you don't see this page, change the **View by** option in the upper-right corner to **Category**.)

3. Click the program you want to delete, and then click **Uninstall**.

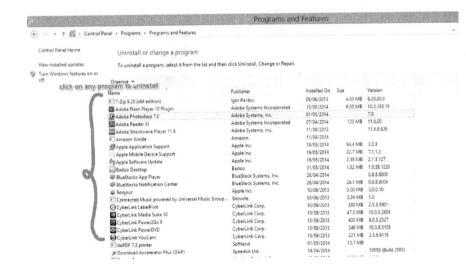

c) Run fewer programs at the same time

If your PC runs at a crawling pace while you're using it, check how many programs you have running at the same time. Each program you run uses up a part of the pc's memory and this will have a huge impact on it's overall performance.

Sometimes, having multiple instances of a program (such as several open email messages) or multiple versions of a program type (more than one antivirus program) can use up memory.

Whenever you receive email messages, try as much as possible to respond to them and close the messages right away. Where possible, keep open only the programs that are absolutely necessary for the task you're working at any given time.

Do this simple step and you will definitely observe an improved performance from your computer.

d) Install ReadyBoost

While the previous step encourages you to close any programs you're not actively using, the fact remains that you might need to use those programs within a few minutes of closing them down.

The solution to this scenario is **ReadyBoost**, a mightily helpful tool that can use the extra space on a flash card or USB storage device to speed up your PC.

All you need to do is to plug in a compatible storage device and then click **Speed up my system** when the AutoPlay dialog box appears on your monitor.

This will also reduce the downtime you experience on your computer.

e) **Troubleshoot and Diagnose**

If your PC is running along smoothly and all of a sudden, it slows down significantly, you need to run a full system virus scan right away. When you do this and your antivirus does not detect any viruses, try updating your antivirus program (if there are any updates available) and perform the virus scan again.

If there any viruses still, then proceed to the troubleshooter tool on your PC. To run the troubleshooter tool, perform the following steps:

1. Click the **Start** button, and then click **Control Panel**.

2. In the search box, type **Troubleshooting**, and then click **Troubleshooting** in the list of results.

3. Under **Systems and Security**, click **Check for performance issues or Run Maintenance Tasks**.

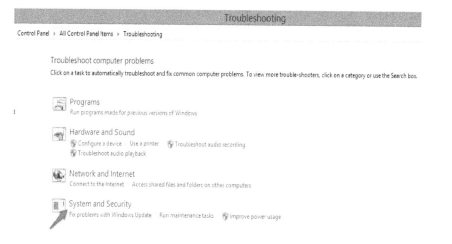

4. Run the Performance troubleshooter or Maintenance Troubleshooter by clicking **Next** in the lower-right corner of the box that shows up.

   Let the tool do its thing and it will resolve any potential issues responsible for the drop in speed of your computer.

f) Perform Disk Cleanup on your hard drive

The longer the period of time that you have been using your PC, the greater the number of software/programs you have installed on it and consequently the more services you're running. Closing a program doesn't always close the service.

That's why merely rebooting your computer helps to fix so many issues that arise because restarting your pc clears out the memory.

You should always perform a Disk Cleanup on your computer hard disk to remove temporary internet files and clear off any other system files you don't need. To do this step, proceed thus:

1. Click the **Start** button, type **Disk Cleanup** in the search box, and then click **Disk Cleanup** in the list of results.

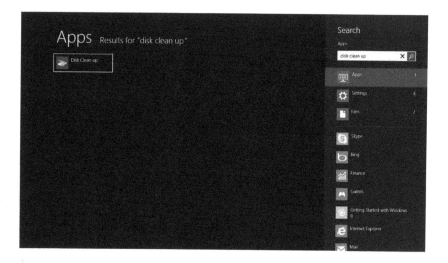

2. After the utility runs, you'll see how much disk space you can free up.

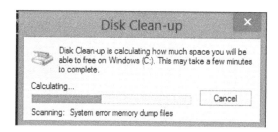

3. Click **OK**, and then click **Delete Files**.

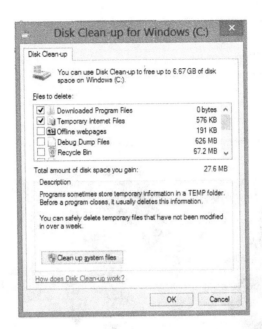

g) **Assess the condition of your hardware**

If after performing all of the above steps, your computer is still running slow, then perhaps you need to inspect the Windows Experience Index of your pc.

This is a rating system of your PC based on five key components. Now, depending on the particular hardware installed on your system, you might need to buy a new PC or simply carry out some hardware upgrades. If you wish to check your computer's Windows Experience Index, do the following:

1. Click the **Start** button, type **Performance Information and Tools** in the search box, and then click **Performance Information and Tools** in the list of results.

2. Click **Re-run the assessment** in the lower-right corner of the window.

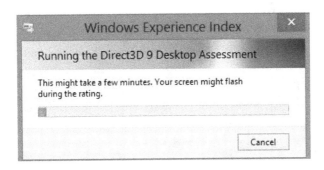

3. Check out your base score. If your score is lower than 3, it might be time to consider a new PC.

h) **Update your PC always**

One of the stress-free ways to protect your PC is to set up your pc to get automatic updates from Microsoft. If you use Windows and other Microsoft software, such as Microsoft Office or Windows Live Essentials, then it is an absolute must that you use the automatic Microsoft Update service.

Performing this step will guarantee that you are also notified about new Microsoft software that you can download for free.

If you want to turn on the automatic updates, visit the **Microsoft Update website**.

i) Change the visual effects settings

Your installed Windows programs has some visually stunning effects which make for an overall pleasant working experience when you're using it.

However, the downside to this is that it can hinder your computer's speed. So if you wish to have a speedy pc, you will have to compromise on the visual display by changing the settings for the appearance of Windows on your computer.

To do this, follow these steps;

1. Click on the **Start** button, type in **Performance Information and Tools** in the search box, and then click **Performance Information and Tools** in the list of results.

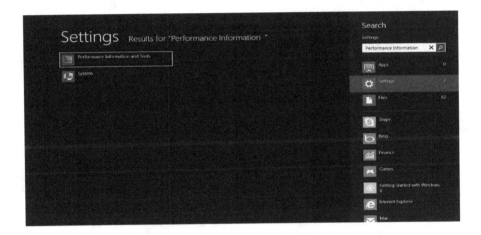

2. Click **Adjust visual effects**.

3. Here you can decide if you want to let Windows choose what's best for your computer, adjust for best appearance, or adjust for best performance.

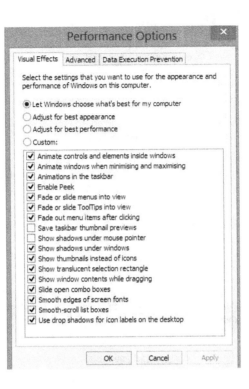

j) **Just shutdown.**

Just by shutting down your pc and rebooting it, you will perform one of the simplest steps towards speeding up your pc. Anytime you do a cold reboot on your computer, any computer program that is still hoarding the computer's memory resources will be forced to release them thereby freeing up even more of your machine's memory for use by other programs.

Even when you do a warm restart on your pc, some of the memory drivers and other core programs will still not be released by the programs that they had been allocated to.

The computer has to be completely shut down and then restarted. This is how it works; whenever you click or start a particular program on your computer, a certain percentage of your computer's memory is allocated to it by the operating system which enables you to use that program for as long as it remains open.

This memory allocated to that particular program is no longer available for use by any other programs. Many programs normally release this allocated memory space when the program is closed but there are some other programs that do not. This occurs largely due to a programming error referred to as a memory leak.

One can suspect a memory leak is at work when a program uses up an abnormally high amount of resources than it usually does. The best way to resolve this is to terminate or end the process, but some processes and core processes cannot be closed.

Shutting down the system will make the operating system forget which memory locations aren't free for use, and so the next time you reboot your pc, all of the installed memory locations will be free to use. This will also boost your speed.

k) Empty the Recycle Bin.

When you delete a program or file on your computer, it is merely sent to the Recycle Bin which is just another temporary holding area on the hard drive designed to make it easy for you to restore deleted files.

To further boost your speed, you have to empty your recycle bin frequently.

Do ensure that you inspect all the contents of your recycle bin before emptying it. Once its been emptied, the space on the hard drive that the data on the bin used to occupy is now available for use by other files.

It is noteworthy that this particular will only marginally boost your computer speed if the hard disk on your pc is almost full.

l) Run "Disk De-fragment" on your hard disk.

Right-click a drive icon in "My Computer" and select "Properties" followed by "Tools". Choose "De-fragment" to let the utility clean up fragmented files and consolidate free space on the drive.

Note: this is not needed on an SSD drive. Defragmentation should be done at least once per week, or more often if the PC is used heavily. Some versions of Windows allow for the scheduling of this utility, and in those cases could be set to run automatically without you ever having to manually run again.

This process may take anywhere from several minutes to an hour or more to complete depending on size of the drive(s) and amount of unused capacity or free space. Consider starting the defragment process so that it will run over night or prior to logging off.

After completion, you should observe an increased speed of hard drive. There are also stand-alone defragmenting programs available from other developers available for download that may or may not charge a fee for use.

A very good example of a free defrag program that allows automatic and scheduled defragmenting is IOBit's Smart Defrag 2.

m) Install anti-virus software and keep it current.

These days, an anti-virus software is absolutely mandatory. Not having one installed would be sheer carelessness. While this step might seem rather obvious, you would be amazed at the number of pc users who don't have an anti-virus program installed or who do not bother to update the program at all.

There are many anti-virus programs to choose from but there are a few free ones are pretty decent.

Some of these include some very popular ones like Avast!, AVG, and Avira AntiVir to mention a few. They each contain the normal virus definition database files which need to be updates regularly so that newest virus programs can be detected by the anti-virus program.

Note that while installing antivirus software actually slows down your computer, it does not slow it down as much as a virus would. Install an Ad Blocker or Malware Bytes to guard against malware and also reduce temp disk space for the browser to a significant extent.

n) Delete Temporary Files.

Temporary Files are used for supporting some applications for a limited period of time and left unused for later. Go to

"C:\Documents and Settings\<username>\Local Settings\Temp" (Windows XP),

"C:\Users\<username>\AppData\Local\Temp" (Windows Vista), or "%TEMP%" (any version of Windows) and delete all the files from this folder.

If there is a problem deleting one or more files, skip those files and remove the rest. This will free a lot of space on the drive. The Temporary Internet Files directory can also be emptied.

0) Clean Up the Primary Partition on your disk.

To do this, perform the following tasks;

Click "Start" type "cleanmgr" and press "Enter" key. Select your primary partition (Windows installed drive, in most cases C:/ drive) and scan it for junk files.

After few seconds, it will show a list of unnecessary files and simply select all these check boxes and start cleaning your drive.

p) **Download a Secure Computer Cleaner.**
Many programs can clean out your computer and delete Junk Files and fix Registry Errors. Some programs are AVG PC Tuneup, AVG QuickTune, CCleaner, RegClean Pro, SpeedyPC Pro, etc.

The Best Free PC Optimizers

While Microsoft Windows is a wonderful bit of software, it is not perfect and neither is it self-sufficient in itself. Hence the need for certain third party software programs to perform some maintenance tasks on the computer.

If your PC is running slowly, and it takes a long time for it to boot up, there are some 3rd party software tools that can help remedy the situation. These utility software tools are an affordable way of making your PC faster and more efficient.

Downloading a PC system utilities tool can help bring life back to your PC. No matter the condition of your pc, whether it is completely broken or is just a bit slow, most of the PC optimizers available today can help you optimise the performance of your computer.

The modus operandi of many of these tools involves clearing all unwanted files, fixing the registry and defragmenting the hard drives on your system.

There are several of these types of tools available for sale but the one you settle for should have all the right features that will ensure a faster operating speed for your pc. Many also have both automatic and manual settings so you can keep your system running smoothly without you having to monitor it constantly.

Microsoft Windows has a disk cleanup tool but it has a little limitation. It can only eliminate temporary internet files but it can't fix all registry errors or organize startup programs. The best way to clean your system is to use a PC optimizer.

Using a PC optimizer to clean your system is quite easy for anyone with any level of experience to use safely without any issues.

As stated earlier, your choice of pc optimiser should have certain features. Here are some features to look out for in a PC optimizer software;

Effectiveness in Repair & Recovery

This refers to the ability of the software to actually fix the problem. You want a program that can actually do what it says on the box, so to speak.

You'll also want the program to be able to recover any lost data, allows you to securely delete files and unwanted programs.
Above all, your tool of choice must be easy to use if you want to be able to use it successfully. Pick one that has a robust user guide and tutorials for new users. Automatic scanning and problem detection/resolution would also be nice features to have.

Diagnostics

In order to find out why your computer is running slowly, you'll need to run a diagnostic scan of your whole system. Some programs run quick and full scans, and some don't run scans at all. Find a program that will fully analyze your computer.

The best PC maintenance software allows you to control automatic or manual scans of your computer to diagnose and monitor hard drive failure, hardware failure, drivers and system information.

Optimization

Once you fix errors and speed up your system, the best utility software will prevent future problems with your PC. Managing startup programs can really help keep your computer running quickly.

Your computer cleanup software should also perform regular maintenance tasks like defragmenting your hard drive, optimizing memory, updating Windows and monitoring internet settings.

Help & Support

When learning how to speed up your computer, you might need some extra help from the software manufacturer. Many have FAQs pages so you can learn how to use more functions of the software.

You should also look for email and live chat features so you can easily reach support representatives. An important feature to notice is how many computers one license covers. If you can find a license that can be applied to 3 or more computers, you'll definitely be saving money.

In order to keep your Windows PC in the best shape possible, use a PC system utilities tool to fix problems and to prevent problems in the future. If you keep your PC clean and working properly, it'll last much longer and keep more money in your wallet.

There are a couple of free PC optimizers that I have been using, and to be honest, almost every free PC optimizer is useless which should not come as a surprise.

However, there are a couple of softwares that works quite well and can stand head to head with some of the paid PC optimizers.

Here is an overview of the best free PC optimizers from my experience;

Wise Care 365 is a complete PC optimizer and maintenance collection. This software tool has quite a few features which catch the eye which include registry cleaner, a disk cleaner and other system utilities that are useful for optimizing your PC.

It's pretty incredible that this software is free because its better off than many paid PC optimizer. There's a Pro version available for Wise Care 365, but the free version has almost all the features available in the Pro version.

Advanced SystemCare 7 Free from IObit is another pretty good software. It's got features that can fix registry errors, boost your system speed and also detect Spyware and Adware. The scanner is not as fast as Wise Care 365, but that's the only major difference between the two of them.

Advanced SystemCare 6 also has a Pro version with more improved features, but for doing your basic pc maintenance, the free version works great. Advanced SystemCare 6 Free is trusted by millions of PC users worldwide.

CCleaner is not an all-in-one PC optimizer, but if you are looking for a stable and easy-to-use system cleaner, you should check out CCleaner. It's really an advanced version of the Windows built-in Disk Cleanup tool and many Windows users like this third party tool.

It's not necessary to use CCleaner if you already got a PC optimizer installed, but if you just want to remove temporary internet files and delete unused registry entries, CCleaner is a great choice.

It's necessary to give your PC a good cleanup once in a while. Many people don't care about PC optimization and maintenance, but doing it can prevent bigger errors from happening and also extend your PC's life.

If you're on a budget, downloading any of the above-mentioned tools wouldn't be a bad idea but if you find that none of the above tools can fix your computer's problem, it might be necessary for you to upgrade or test a more advanced software such as Advanced System Optimizer from Systweak.

But of course if a free tool works for you, then you should stick to it by all means.

A few others worth checking out are –

System Mechanic Pro,

Fix-It Utilities Pro and

WinOptimizer.

These are some of the best PC system utilities tools for getting your machine up to speed.

RECOMMENDED RESOURCES

Don't Lose Your Digital Life. Back Up All Your Data, Music & Photos Files For FREE
http://bit.ly/freedatabackup

Fix The Blue Screen Of Death On Your Pc - http://bit.ly/FixBlueScreenOfDeath

Computer Repair Video Course - Learn How To Repair Your Computer & save Money On Costly Repairs And Even Start Your Own Business http://bit.ly/ComputerRepairMastery

Laptop Repair Made Easy (Hd Video Series) - Laptop Repair Made Easy Is A Complete High Definition Video Series On How To Repair Laptops For Fun Or Profit
http://bit.ly/LaptopRepairMadeEasy

Lcd Monitor Repair Made Easy - How To Repair Lcd Monitors With Step-by-step Videos -
http://bit.ly/LcdMonitorRepairMadeEasy

Filecure - Instantly Fixes All Types Of Broken Or Unknown File Extensions Including Unknown Email Attachments, Archived And Compressed Files, Audio And Music Files, Document Files, Internet Downloads, Graphic Files, Movies Videos, Multimedia Files, And More - http://bit.ly/FileCure101

Regcure - #1 Registry Cleaner. - http://bit.ly/RegCureClean

Best Data Recovery Software - Data Recovery Software Products for All Windows and Mac Computers - http://bit.ly/DataRecoverySoftware

Xoftspyse - Clean Spyware Instantly - The New And Improved Xoftspyse Is The Most Powerful Anti-spyware Program Yet. Promote This Fresh New Gui, A Suite Of Advanced Features, The Largest Spyware Detection Database, Lighting Fast Free Scan - http://bit.ly/Xoftspy

Scan And Fix Windows Errors Fast - Thoroughly Scans Your PC For Errors. One Click And PC Unleashed Fixes Them All. Tools To Repair And Optimize - http://bit.ly/FixWindowsErrorsFast

Table of Contents

www.ingramcontent.com/pod-product-compliance
Lightning Source LLC
Chambersburg PA
CBHW060936050326
40689CB00013B/3110